modern comfort

modern comfort

text by
Katherine Sorrell

Photography by Fabian Björnstjerna
and Stellan Herner

ROCKPORT

First published in North America by
Rockport Publishers, Inc.
33 Commercial Street
Gloucester, Massachusetts 01930-5089
telephone: (978) 282-3505
facsimile: (978) 283-2742
www.rockpub.com

First published in Great Britain in 2000 by
Conran Octopus Limited
A part of Octopus Publishing Group
2-4 Heron Quays, London E14 4JP

The original edition of this book was published
under the title *R.O.O.M. B.O.O.K.* in 1997 by
Probono Publishing, Stockholm. The concept was
based on the design philosophy of Hans Axelsson
and Klas Litzen, founders of the R.O.O.M. shops;
and the work of Lars and Ulla Walles, textile
designers and interior decorators.

Art Director & Project Leader: Marie Walerud

Photographers of the Home Settings:

Fabian Björnstjerna and Stellan Herner

Stylist: Lotta Noremark

Text and research for the original edition: Bengt Åkesson

British Library Cataloguing-in-Publication Data.
A catalogue record for this book is available
from the British Library.

ISBN 1-56496-709-3

Printed in China

contents

the softer side of modern living

These days, we pay more attention than ever before to the design of our homes; ironically, though, we have less time than ever before in which to enjoy spending time in them. And not only that: we also want them to perform an almost impossible number of tasks – serving not just as a living space, but also as an office, a place for entertaining, somewhere to gather the family together and a quiet spot in which to relax alone. Clearly, a new attitude is needed to decorating, one that understands the need for function while paying attention to the equally important need for self-indulgence, one that transcends the boundaries of the traditional but is not an unthinking slave to the whims of fashion.

More than just a 'look', modern comfort is all about creating a home that is both practical and pleasurable; that works on a physical level, of course, but that also has emotional qualities, that is welcoming and nurturing, and that has personality and soul.

Neither relentlessly minimal nor fussily over-adorned, this softer contemporary style balances good looks with the demands of our everyday lives. A few key elements are ever-present:

a consistent palette of natural materials, for example, has attractive authenticity as well as timeless durability. Following on from this, texture (the grain of wood, the sheen of stainless steel, the warmth of wool) is as important as colour, which is limited to muted, mostly matt shades with the occasional use of vibrant contrasts. Furniture and storage pieces are flexible and adaptable; the former streamlined but also soft and supportive, the latter capacious and understated. Lighting, too, is flexible, capable of general illumination, specific tasks and setting a particular mood. And, finally, accessories are expressive and interesting, beautiful to look at and satisfying to use.

In this book we show a selection of real rooms that are effortlessly attractive and very much for living in. Not rigorous but realistic, they all express their owners' careful planning and inspired sense of aesthetics, making the most of space and light, combining textures, shapes and colours to irresistible effect and demonstrating that instinct is every bit as important as following the rules. And many of their ideas are straightforward to emulate or adapt without spending huge amounts of money – it's often the thoughtful details that count for the most. So, look to *Modern Comfort* for both luxury and logic – the results, as seen here, are convenient and comfortable, inviting, appealing and full of impact.

1 A subtle combination within a limited, harmonious colour palette gives a room easy and elegant simplicity. Here the warm hue and beautiful grain of polished natural wood draw the eye immediately; the rougher, more casual style of the floorboards is an interesting and attractive foil to the furniture. Some sleek upholstery, an understated modern light and a single-stem flower are all that's needed to complete the look

living rooms

Multifunctional spaces for enjoying

We demand a great deal from our living rooms. A sociable area for chatting with friends or family. A quiet corner for reading, thinking, listening to music. A play space for children. A functional work environment for letter-writing, sewing, studying. A stress-free spot in which to do absolutely nothing. We want it to be all these things and, as if that weren't enough, to look good, too.

Use unfussy furniture, understated colours and plenty of storage to create a room that feels spacious, calm and inviting.

Creating a living room that can adapt to all the requirements of modern living while being comfortable and convenient is a matter of careful planning – but it's by no means as difficult as it may seem. Think in terms of essential building blocks, but let your instincts guide you, too; a room that's easy and attractive is the result of personality, not rules.

The first consideration is function. Prioritize areas for different activities, and ensure that it's easy to move around the room and that the arrangement works for solitude, small groups of people and perhaps larger parties as well. You may have just one focal point (traditionally the fireplace, more recently the television) or several (a work of art, a view from a window or a beautiful piece of furniture).

Next, plan your lighting. You need not only good general light, but also lights for reading and working by, and lights that create a pleasant mood – especially important for relaxing alone or with guests.

1 This sociable arrangement of sofas has an attractive geometry that is restful and tidy. The all-natural tones and textures offer a pleasing, gentle unity, while a pair of African baskets and fresh flowers inject a dash of personality.

Unify your scheme by painting muted shades on walls and employing the natural tones of wood or sisal underfoot. Avoid clutter by allowing for generous storage, and choose furniture that has strong, clean shapes but is so well upholstered that you can't wait to sink into it. Mix textures rather than colours or patterns for a sophisticated, modern look, and add a few hand-crafted accessories to soften the overall effect. For a feeling of spaciousness, effortless order, calm and repose, all these are straight-forward, achievable ideas, resulting in a room that's a delightful place in which you will want to spend time.

2 A quiet reading area where supportive armchairs, a well-positioned light and an absence of vivid colours ensure calm repose. An adjustable, hinged-arm lamp would make an excellent alternative to this simple style.

3 The strict, precise lines of this square display cavity are ultra-modern; it is effective because it has been so well executed. Contrasted with the wooden floorboards and a rustic metal and wicker lamp, it makes a surprising and interesting element in a room.

4 + **5** For general light, recessed halogen spotlights are excellent – bright, flexible and unobtrusive. But it's also nice to add fittings with character: here, for example, a crook-shaped wall light makes an unusual statement (especially when reflected infinitely in two mirrors) and, while one aluminium, office-style pendant is attractive, a whole row of them has real panache. When planning lighting, don't forget that a dimmer switch allows you to alter the atmosphere of a room with ease.

6 The daring contrast between this sofa and these chairs, in terms of their shape, colour and texture, works so well because the colours of the walls and floor have been kept entirely neutral.

light, bright and airy
– a look that's relaxed
and sophisticated

Can a living room be more inviting than this? A set of matching sofas and chairs arranged in a symmetrical group could easily appear uptight and rigid, but here their uniformity of shape and colour is a pleasing foil to squashy upholstery and bright scatter cushions, resulting in a look that is both sophisticated and refreshingly relaxed.

Despite the close grouping and solid forms of the furniture, the pale colours and the consistency of materials used throughout this room give it a strong feeling of light and space. Parchment-coloured voile blinds in the simplest of styles gently filter sunshine, while walls in a soft putty shade emphasize airiness without the harshness of brilliant-white paint. The natural wood of the bookshelf and picture frames echoes the grain of the

parquet floor, its golden tone complemented by a large sisal rug that's neat, clean and understated. Simple everyday objects such as a basket of fruit and a selection of favourite books become bright focal points in a setting of such subtle elegance. By day bright and welcoming, by night this room becomes a warm, cosy sanctuary, a retreat from the outside world and a space that is perfect for informal entertaining.

1 Loose covers are informal and highly practical, even in such a pale colour (though darker shades or subtle patterns would look equally as good). They can be taken off and thrown in the washing machine, and will wear attractively with age.

2 (Overleaf) Any more furniture and this room might look cluttered. As it is, the owner has stamped his personality on it while maintaining a look that is strong and fresh.

3

5 The oak floor running from hall to living room makes this house seem more open and cohesive, while the addition of the sisal rug is a good way to define the seating area. It provides a wonderful contrast of textures, too, from cool, smooth wood to crunchy woven matting – a real treat for bare feet.

3 A monochromatic colour scheme gives instant impact, and has the advantage of being easy to contrast or coordinate with.

4 This reading lamp is a perfect example of the Modernist ethos that 'form follows function'. With a heavy, stable base, it is infinitely adjustable and will look good in almost any room.

4

6 This living room takes on a completely different character at night. The warm colours of the natural materials used come into their own, enhanced by a judicious arrangement of table lamps, which can, of course, be moved at will. The tour de force, however, is the massing of numerous candles, adding vitality, drama and an instinctive sense of well-being.

7 A single candle can look mean, but grouping several together is much more satisfying. Choose the scented variety and emphasize the mood with a soothing aroma.

23

beautiful basics
offer a functional
solution

Get the basics right and your living room will function efficiently, look attractive and feel like a good place to be. The owners of this spacious apartment, for example, have ensured that their second living room is an enjoyable and practical environment for working (the desk is positioned by the window to make the most of natural light), painting (an easel placed in

a corner, similarly, takes advantage of the large windows) or simply settling down for a good read.

Counterpointing the soft, rounded shapes of the chairs and footstools, a massive set of cube-shaped book shelves makes a dramatic visual statement. Using an entire wall for storage is often a more convenient and attractive choice than placing smaller units around the room. The only supplementary storage needed is a classic butler's tray – handy when moving from room to room – and a large, country-style log basket, for holding newspapers and magazines.

1 Though the colours used here are muted and natural, the look is anything but bland, thanks to the contrasts between gloss and matt paintwork, smooth wood and rough sisal flooring, and the heavy canvas covers of the chairs against the filmy voile of the blinds.

2 (Overleaf) Don't be afraid to mix classic and contemporary pieces. Loose covers in a modern fabric update traditional furniture, while the clean lines of a contemporary bookcase complement those of an elegant floor lamp that was designed in the Thirties.

4

3 Lifting furniture off the floor
(in this room, even the bookshelves
are hung above the skirting board)
creates an almost subliminal feeling
of extra space.

4 Access to high-level storage
should always be a consideration,
especially when it is used regularly.
Another way of making the most
of shelves such as these would
be to alternate the books with an
occasional piece of glassware
or pottery.

the harmony of
natural textures and
a neutral palette

For unfussy harmony in a room, even where several different styles of furniture are placed together, there's no doubt that the colours of nature are unfailingly attractive. It's a straightforward premise: take a palette of cream, ivory and stone, and combine it with unpainted wood, wicker, sisal, canvas and muslin. As demonstrated overleaf, the effect is airy and easygoing, neither too formal nor too casual.

Providing one or two points of brighter colour overcomes any possibility of the neutral tones becoming monotonous. Here, the unexpected touches – two subtle, one more exuberant – take the form of a woollen border to the sisal rug, a couple of lemon-yellow lampshades and a large, very vivid modern collage. These help, too, to reinforce the secondary motif that underlies the arrangement of this room: a strong structure of horizontal and vertical lines that, together with the subtle tones and natural materials, gives it logic and cohesion.

1 A length of sheer printed muslin, pierced with eyelets and threaded onto a slim metal pole, is much less fussy than traditional curtains. As an alternative you could use curtain clips, or simply sew a deep casing through which the pole could be passed. The wooden louvres behind give extra privacy at night.

2 The muted colours of this room are extremely restful; a brighter touch such as the yellow lampshades is fun, and can be replaced with alternative styles whenever you feel like a change. You could also add several cushions in different colours if you wanted more variety.

3 Practical and attractive in an understated way, this radiator cover has been designed to echo the horizontal lines of the louvred blind above it. It also makes a useful shelf.

5

4 The disparate styles of a modern coffee table, rustic chair, plump, upholstered sofa and Regency side table work well together because of their similar materials and colours. They all demonstrate a simplicity of form that not only echoes that of the entire room, but also ensures that they would work in practically any setting.

5 Shallow shelves such as these allow the owners to display their favourite (and best-looking) books and CDs. Think of shelving as an alternative to hanging a picture, and remember that you can always hide your more prosaic titles behind cupboard doors.

using favourite objects for an individual touch

1 Well-loved, handmade pieces, however inexpensive, add character to any room. A certain intensity of colour and depth of shine, as well as an endearing round form, give this simple jug, for example, huge appeal. It might not be part of a matching set, but its colour coordinates perfectly with the room, and offsets beautifully the finer (though still rather quaint) crockery with which it is used.

Sometimes, or perhaps especially, in the most contemporary of settings a careful selection of hand-crafted accessories can make a wonderful display. Or even better, as here, they can be used on a daily basis, giving pleasure not only in terms of their shape and colour, but also because of their weight, their surface texture and the way they feel when being used.

In this nineteenth-century house, charmingly old-fashioned radiators and architraves have been painted glossy white to complement the matt, slightly off-white walls. These, together with a warm wooden parquet floor, provide a timelessly elegant background against which it would be possible to place practically any type of furniture. The owner has, in fact, chosen an eclectic but relaxed mix of pieces – a classic sofa, a chic Regency side table, a pared-down modern lamp and a library table with the legs sawn off which acts as a coffee table – placed apparently haphazardly, but actually with great concern for convenience and maximizing the available space.

Dotted around are a variety of interesting pieces, from the robust, pot-bellied cream jug and the sculpture and pottery displayed on the window ledge to the artworks on the walls. Even the tasselled cushions underline the quality that makes this room so successful – a feeling of real personality, of ease and of true joie de vivre.

½ PINT MUG

2 Not overtly modern in style, this room is, nevertheless, modern in aesthetic. Light, airy and uncluttered, it contains a confident choice of mismatching pieces – a combination of family heirlooms, bargain finds, high-street purchases, and personal treasures. The colour scheme appears effortless but is painstakingly precise, with pattern restricted to the cushions, making a vibrant, striking focal point.

3 Use a generously sized, hand-painted bowl for serving food and you'll double the pleasure of dining. This example has been chosen to complement the room's colours.

creating contrast
with colour, texture
and pattern

Rooms that are uncluttered, contain simple shapes and use a palette of just a few soft colours are always the most restful. Not, however, when they tend towards the look and feel of a monastic cell, which is why some strictly minimalist rooms may at first sight seem appealing but are in fact extremely uncomfortable to live in. In this large living room, the sparsity of the all-white upholstery and pale, streamlined tables could have been inhibiting, but it is tempered by some cosier additions – tasselled cushions in broad, bold stripes, a collection of fat beeswax candles and a wicker basket and dish. These last two objects pick up the texture of the woven sisal rug, which in turn provides a contrast to the smooth limed-oak floorboards and the slabs of natural stone. The overall result is one of gentle, subtle variety.

A key feature of this house is its sleek, contemporary furniture. Beside a squashy, roomy sofa and upholstered stools at one end of the living room are wooden tables that are simple but well made, while the lamps on them are similarly unfussy and sophisticated. At the other end of the room a leather and chrome chair (a twentieth-century classic by Modernist architect Le Corbusier) has an imposing, sculptural presence, but also makes a luxurious spot for a quiet read.

1 The open weave of pure, natural linen is crisp and elegant, and these cushions have been loosely stuffed so that they're exceptionally comfortable. Spicy colours look particularly warm against the cool, strong tones of the rest of the room.

2 (Overleaf) One way to emphasize a room's size is to keep all the furniture fairly low and simple in shape. Here, this theory is reinforced by the strong horizontals of each piece, including the custom-made radiator cover and the folds of the sheer roman blind.

3 + **4** An intriguing grid-like pattern is established by this unusual banister and the frame of this cubic Le Corbusier armchair. Combining leather with metal softens the hard edges while retaining a strong, structural feel. Reflective surfaces, such as chrome, smooth wood, even the slightly dimpled black hide of the chair, maximize the abundance of daylight in this bright, sunny room.

3

4

layering white on white for ultimate subtlety

When your aim is a sense of airiness and cool, calm repose, you can't beat the purity of white on white. Against a backdrop of limed-oak floorboards, white-painted woodwork and a row of white geraniums in white pots, this large, squashy sofa, topped with white cushions and throws, makes the ultimate retreat for relaxing, reading or gazing at the stars at night.

Of course, there's more than just one shade of white. Modern brilliant blue-white, for example, can appear flat and sterile, and is usually best avoided. It's a simple enough job, however, to mix it with a small amount of ochre pigment to create an off-white that has far more character. Soft, creamy whites look natural and feel familiar and comfortable; they work well with both pale and dark shades and with the natural tones of wood and wicker, as seen here. Their versatility allows them to be played up or down – combine with charcoal, chocolate or taupe for a sophisticated, restrained effect or, for a relaxed and easy look such as the one achieved in this appealing sitting room, use with a brighter colour such as sky blue, apple green or sunshine yellow.

1 White on white is the ultimate in muted colour palettes. It's a look that's easy to achieve and extremely effective, especially when dappled by fresh winter sunlight.

2 (Overleaf) Choosing pale colours makes the most of a sunny aspect. Keeping to simple patterns – a checked rug, striped chair cover and cushions with a subtle snowflake design – enhances the reflective atmosphere.

46

offices

Creative workspaces for the home

It may once have been a spare bedroom, a dining room or even the cupboard under the stairs; today it's likely to have become a home office, fully fitted with all the paraphernalia required to carry out a demanding full- or part-time job.

Just because an office needs to be efficient and functional, however, doesn't mean that it can't also be inviting and comfortable. This is your

Your work environment should reflect your personality as well as your professionalism. A comfortable chair, spacious desk, good lighting and efficient storage will allow you to concentrate on the task in hand.

chance to liberate yourself from dull work surroundings and create a space that's as enjoyable as any other room in the house.

Four key elements govern the structure of any home office. Your seat must be supportive and stable. Your desk should be at the right height and large enough to spread out all your documents. Lights should be adjustable and bright. And, lastly, it's essential to provide ample storage so that you can maintain uncluttered surroundings.

None of these features, however, need be monotonous, mass-produced echoes of the standard office. Why shouldn't your desk be a block of beautifully grained wood, cut with a soft curve to be ergonomic and easy on the eye? Or a sheet of toughened glass, rested on either polished-metal filing cabinets or trestles painted an interesting colour? Your shelves could be an old kitchen dresser or a bright plastic unit on wheels, your lighting

1 Well-organized storage makes a home office look – and feel – more professional. Open shelves work well for tidy and attractive files, and you can hide messier stationery, accounts, computer paraphernalia and so on behind closed doors. Here, sandblasted glass acts as a good screen yet still appears smart and airy.

an antique Anglepoise or a sleek Italian desk lamp. Be flexible: squeeze an office space into the corner of a living room or bedroom, hiding it with a screen that has built-in shelving. Whatever the room's layout and style, though, add personality with favourite paintings, handmade crafts or a simple vase of flowers. Think laterally, and the results will not only perform well when you're working under pressure, but also bring unexpected – and very welcome – pleasure.

2 There's no reason why an office chair has to be metal or plastic. If you prefer the appearance of natural wood, this style satisfies all the performance requirements while providing a reassuringly traditional feel.

3 An adjustable lamp is a huge bonus in a home office. Always position it so that it doesn't reflect onto your computer screen.

4 If you use your office only occasionally, there's no reason why you shouldn't sit on a supportive domestic chair. If, however, you use your workspace a great deal, choose a model that adjusts to your height and working posture – there are various good-looking models around, as shown by this example.

55

organization and versatility – essentials for a successful office

Build in as much adaptability as you can to the design of your home office and it will pay off enormously. Choose chairs, storage units, even tables on castors (some types can be locked for stability), so they can be moved around without any effort. Purchase lamps that can be tilted at different heights and angles, giving you the option to work wherever you want without eye strain. And fit storage that provides ample space, with shelves at different heights and a variety of clearly labelled boxes, cabinets and trays (these can be moved around, too), so you won't be distracted by mess or waste time trying to find things.

Such planning is the key to a successful home office, but it's not the only essential: paying attention to the look and feel of the room is equally important. In this small office, formerly a spare bedroom, for example, there's a cosy, domestic atmosphere, despite the filing cabinets, the efficient rows of shelves and the neatly placed computer equipment. The colour and texture of old wooden floorboards are complemented by the unfussy wooden desk and shelves, the seat is a dining chair covered in off-white canvas and the equipment is a mix of old and new, combining function with familiarity. Although full, the room seems spacious and airy because it's so well organized and, bathed in natural light, it has a calm and welcoming feel.

1 A hinged-arm lamp throws out good light and can be moved to different working areas. This modern version is the epitome of simplicity and, with its soft matt metal, is not too harsh looking for a home environment.

2 (Overleaf) How many hi-tech corporate offices are as appealing as this? Everything's in its place, and the L-shaped desk provides plenty of workspace. A view is a bonus, too – as long as it doesn't distract you from your work.

3 (Overleaf) Office equipment tends to be bland and boring, but if you surround yourself with a personal choice of objects, they will add interest to your space and to your working day.

home-working made easier with character and comfort

If you work from home you may well find that you spend more time in your office than any other room in the house. So it makes sense to have things around that give you pleasure – a vase of flowers, elegant coffee mugs and water tumblers, a wooden desk with an attractive grain, attractive colours and funky but functional lights.

The office shown on these pages is in a home/work building; desks and storage are in one large room at the far end of the kitchen-sitting room, while at the other end a dining room is also used for meetings. It's a flexible environment that's deliberately far removed from the conventional office. The feel is both fresh and tranquil, thanks to the carefully chosen furniture, the expanses of uncluttered surfaces and the varying tones of muted green. Such easy-to-achieve features, although purely functional, add undeniable character and life, giving the impression that this is an extremely enjoyable space in which to spend one's working day.

1 Brighten an office desk with a vase of fresh flowers and mix business with pleasure in an instant. These tulips have been chosen carefully to complement the colours in the office, while the simple glass vase in which they've been casually arranged makes an eye-catching centrepiece.

2 This room makes a pleasant setting for both eating and meeting. The high ceiling, large windows and plain walls and floor provide a neutral backdrop, while the soft colours and padded chairs add a dash of individuality.

3 A column radiator against a panelled wall and on a wooden floor usually belongs in a traditional living room. Leaving such features unaltered gives a workspace a friendly, informal air.

4 (Overleaf) A busy home/work space is well lit by pendant lamps and well served by storage cupboards that have been adapted from conventional kitchen units. The rooms flow easily into one another but can, for privacy, be separated by pairs of doors.

kitchens &
dining rooms

Integrated spaces for food and conversation

Today's kitchen has become the focal point of the home, providing not only an efficient space for cooking but also a welcoming place for the family to gather, for children to play or do homework, for entertaining friends, doing laundry, watching television and many other activities.

These, then, are the things to think about when designing a kitchen, as well as the essentials of how it will function. The basics are to site the sink,

For a kitchen that both looks good and functions well, choose materials that are hard-wearing and long-lasting: wood, stone, ceramic tiles and stainless steel all have their own attractive authenticity.

cooker and refrigerator, fit in appliances, allocate storage and workspace, and provide good lighting and adequate ventilation. At the same time, though, consider the room's adaptability, appearance and atmosphere. You might, for example, prefer unfitted furniture to fitted, or a combination of both. Open shelves and hanging racks complement built-in cupboards, but won't work unless you're particularly tidy and possess visually pleasing equipment. For extra flexibility, you may need storage units on castors, fold-out tables and stacking chairs or stools. It's enjoyable to eat meals at a large, sturdy table in the centre of the kitchen or, if your home is open-plan, the kitchen can merge seamlessly into the dining area.

Overall, keep the scheme laid-back and simple. With a neutral, natural colour palette it is always possible to add highlights of colour in the form of textiles, utensils or houseplants. And remember that it needn't cost the earth to enhance the room with beautiful handles and taps, an interesting paint colour: a satisfactory solution to both practicalities and aesthetics.

1 In a simple kitchen with white painted cabinets and long runs of open shelving, a plain wooden table with equally understated chairs is all that's required for easy, attractive dining. The pendant lampshades are modern and striking, while their clean lines and soft matt colour ensure that they complement rather than detract from the setting.

when opposites attract: contrasting materials have dramatic impact

The relationship between tones and textures is just as important as the use of colour in a room, and in this family kitchen the interplay between the materials used gives it an extra dimension of interest. Fitted cupboards, faced with cherrywood panels, contrast with drawers fronted with stainless steel: dark and light, grained and smooth, warm and cool, classic and contemporary – such juxtapositions provide unexpected variety, although the carefully planned layout and the chromed handles throughout pull the look together.

There are more contrasts in a sweep of work surface made of shiny steel and dark, cool granite, backed with cheerful yellow tiles. This stretch of wall, the working hub of the kitchen, contains a huge amount of storage, ranging from deep drawers to narrow shelves; it's enclosed but for a drainer and a couple of shelves over the sink, and a wine rack in which the diagonals break up otherwise strong verticals and horizontals. These shapes echo the lines of the quarry-tiled floor, too, which has been elegantly laid at an angle to emphasize the room's spaciousness and irresistibly draw you in.

1 Hanging your best-looking utensils ensures that they're handy when you need them, saves space and provides an attractive display. These stainless steel implements complement the steel-laminate drawer-fronts used elsewhere and glow against the handmade tiles.

2

4 In a large kitchen, the floor is especially important, but you should always choose high-quality, hard-wearing materials that are easy to clean. There are many considerations to bear in mind: these quarry tiles, for example, are attractive and durable, but can be hard on the feet – and on dropped crockery. The same applies to flagstones, brick and ceramic tiles. Although lino, cork and vinyl are warm and soft underfoot, they are not as long-lasting, while wood is a good all-rounder, but easily marks and dents, and requires more maintenance.

2 In black and white, the contrasting qualities of the materials used for the fitted units are demonstrated dramatically. A rush-seated, country-style chair tucked out of the way by the window makes a useful seat, ready for pulling up to the dining table when needed.

3 In perhaps the strongest reiteration of the intriguing contrasts of this kitchen, an old wood-burning stove sits next to a defiantly modern cooker. Though they could hardly be more different in style, each plays an equally important role in this scheme.

3

bold answers for a
small, tricky space

Sometimes, because they've required such careful planning, the smallest or most awkwardly shaped kitchens actually work the best. Here, for example, the owner was faced with a long, narrow space, one side of which backed onto the rounded wall of a stairwell. The solution was to cover the wall with ceramic tiles and onto it, either side of a large-scale cooker, build ranks of open shelves, the lower, larger ones used for pans, the upper ones for crockery and condiments. A hanging rack runs along the tiled wall, and the result is a place for everything and a feel that is busy but not cramped.

On the wall opposite, a more traditional run of units has been fitted below a stainless steel surface. With neutral colours predominating, the walls are painted a fresh mango shade while a free-standing pushbin and fridge/freezer make bold, characterful, colourful statements.

1 There was a time when kitchen fittings were universally box-shaped and known as 'white goods'. Now, however, vibrant colours and unconventional forms are easy to find and deserve to be shown off as interesting objects in their own right. If you long for bright colour but aren't ready to dispose of your white appliance, try transforming its exterior with carefully applied spray paint.

2 Instead of knobs or handles, circular cut-outs add visual appeal to this simple shelving unit.

3 This stainless steel surface looks sleek and professional but requires meticulous cleaning. Other surfaces have their pros and cons: granite, slate and marble are luxurious but expensive; wood is beautiful but needs oiling and keeping dry; tiles are practical but may crack and the grout can trap dirt; manmade solid surfaces such as Corian are good all-rounders but not a 'natural' material; and laminates are practical and inexpensive but may show burns and knife marks. To help you choose, seek out expert advice.

4 The sheer variety of storage in this kitchen is impressive – and also inexpensive to emulate. Everything is to hand, and not even the space below the bottom shelves has been wasted – wicker baskets hold bits and pieces that are used only occasionally. It's always best to store such items in the highest and lowest places, keeping day-to-day utensils within easy reach.

5 + 6 Strong, sturdy kitchen equipment in a classic style is highly functional and has the added advantage of looking good.

7 The colourful fridge-freezer
and pushbin are kept in a side
passage adjacent to the kitchen.
There is just enough room for a
small table (which doubles as an
extra work surface) and chairs, as
well as another shelf unit – this one
deep enough to stack bottles of
wine. A framed blackboard is useful
for jotting down shopping lists,
recipes and reminders.

8 Characterful crockery and
traditional bone-handled cutlery
have a place in every kitchen,
looking good set out on the dinner
table or displayed on open shelving.

thoughtful details and the eternal appeal of open-plan

In one large, airy room a spacious kitchen runs right into an informal dining area, allowing guests and cooks to mingle and chat in a relaxed and convivial manner. Of course, having such a huge open-plan area to play with helps: there'd be no enjoyment if the room was a cramped, stuffy, disorganized mess.

Planning a 'U'-shaped kitchen such as this – and the other classic shapes, 'L', single-lines, galleys and islands – may be a more straightforward job than, say, the narrow, curving kitchen on the previous pages. However, attention to detail is still paramount, as is a little lateral thinking.

The owners of this room decided to dispense with the upper rows of cupboards that are normally seen in fitted kitchens, in favour of sturdy open shelves that match the capacious beech units below. This opens up the room even further, and the pretty ceramics, glasses and utensils on show add colour and personality. A wooden work surface, white-tiled walls and an old-fashioned ceramic sink continue the theme of simple efficiency. In the friendly dining space, a massive scrubbed-oak table is surrounded by unfussy wicker chairs and topped by a minimal metal chandelier. All in all, the open-plan scheme shows a light but intelligent touch that makes for a distinctively spacious and relaxed area for socializing.

1 Where possible, it's nice to position a sink by a window. A swivelling pillar tap, here in a traditional design, is very practical – but do ensure that it is tall enough to allow you to fill large pans with ease.

2 (Overleaf) Limed-oak floorboards extend from kitchen to dining room, unifying the two. A sisal rug beneath the table gives definition to the seating area, its narrow blue border subtly complementing the nautical blue of the chairs, which in turn echoes the spotted and striped crockery on the kitchen shelves.

3 (Pages 86–87) In a kitchen that's full of hard surfaces and neutral colours, the soft texture, interesting patterns and bright shades of rugs and blinds make a welcome addition. When you use textiles in a kitchen, ensure that rugs are non-slip and that any curtains won't flap into food or, worse, brush the flames of a gas hob. Blinds – roman, roller or Venetian – are usually a safer, neater option.

4 The light, loose weave of wicker is highly appropriate in this pale, bright room, and the chandelier makes a decorative focal point. In fact, it looks as good by day as it does when lit at night.

5 An enormous expanse of window allows this dining table to be drenched in light all year round. The folding oak table, in a timeless design, is a simple slab of wood that provides a solid platform for an unpretentious display of crockery, fruit and flowers.

4

mixing old and new with impressive ingenuity

Even in a kitchen that has several hi-tech, ultra-modern features, it's possible to feel comfortably at home. Individually, the structural extractor hood, the almost floor-to-ceiling stainless steel fridge/freezer, the funky appliances, even the bright mosaic tiling in this well-appointed kitchen could appear hard, cold and off-putting. Combined as they are, however, with the warmth of wooden units and floorboards, the informality of open shelves and comfortable, brightly upholstered stools, the overall impression is one of originality and a happy mix of classic styling with new ideas.

It goes to show that it's always worth experimenting, although detailed planning should never be dispensed with. Problems can be turned into assets, as with this cooker hood which, in order to be vented outside, needed a long run of usually unattractive trunking. Rather than conceal it, however, the owner has turned it into the most striking feature of the room. With stainless steel, honey-coloured beech and turquoise predominating, care has been taken not to detract from the kitchen's sleek looks: the shelf displays are restricted to white, blue and clear glass, and anything unsightly has been banished to the lower cupboards. This type of scheme takes discipline but, as demonstrated here, can appear effortless, engaging and inviting.

1 Upholstered kitchen stools can add greatly to a decorative scheme. Stick to plain fabrics or simple checks or stripes: heavy cotton such as this is hard-wearing and easily changed when the mood takes you; you could even use tea towels (a good trick for a small blind, too).

2

2 The bold lines of an extractor hood and its trunking, faced in stainless steel, made a starting point for the design of these well-ordered open shelves. Mosaic is a wonderful alternative to standard tiles, and can be bought in large sheets, making application easy.

3 The brushed stainless steel front of this good-looking cooker complements the metal surfaces elsewhere in the kitchen. Don't overlook details such as knobs, handles and light switches – because you use them so frequently, it's important that they're pleasant to the touch.

3

4 (Overleaf) The items in this kitchen have been chosen because they're basic but beautiful, such as these simple glass tumblers with heavy bases and delicate rims – enjoyable to use and sufficiently attractive to display on open shelves.

5 (Overleaf) A pair of stools can be tucked under the overhanging edge of this island unit. Another practical point is the lighting: recessed spotlights in the ceiling give good overall light, while smaller spots have been fitted beneath the lowest shelf to illuminate the work surfaces. An alternative would be to use strip lights with a baffle to shade glare; either option avoids the problem of shadows cast by using central overhead illumination.

4

flexibility for formal and informal occasions

Adjacent to the innovative kitchen shown on the previous pages, a comfortable dining room continues the theme of using attractive, good-quality materials in interesting ways. The same limed-oak boards that cover the kitchen extend across the whole open-plan room – with the exception of the hearth, which has been laid with slabs of granite. A small section of floor has been cut out and inserted with glass bricks, giving an intriguing view down into the living room below.

The vivid blue of the kitchen tiling has been reiterated in the upholstery of some occasional chairs and in a couple of large pieces of artwork that are casually propped against the walls and on a window ledge. Around the dining area, however, there are only the natural colours of the polished mahogany table and white canvas-covered chairs. Such a neutral scheme allows great flexibility: depending on how it is styled, the setting can be dressed up or down as the occasion dictates – it could easily accommodate a formal meal for eight, for example, but would not be over-imposing for a casual family supper. Instead of hanging a central pendant lamp over the table, a row of spotlights in the ceiling provides discreet illumination, which could easily be supplemented by the atmospheric glow of candlelight.

1 The liming on these new oak boards emphasizes their attractive grain and makes them slightly paler, although still a beautiful golden shade. Inserting glass bricks into the floor is an exciting idea and increases the light available to both this room and the living room below. Before attempting such work, however, it's advisable to consult an architect or structural engineer.

2 White on white, with just the natural tones of oak and mahogany, creates a minimal scheme for this elegant dining area. As such, it's a blank canvas for casual meals or more impressive occasions, depending on how the table is dressed. Zip-up covers on the chairs allow them to be transformed quickly and easily.

3 This barrel chair by architect and designer Frank Lloyd Wright is an exquisite piece that perfectly complements the natural woods and cobalt blues used in the kitchen and dining room.

4 A houseplant, in the simplest of pots, its leaves an interesting shape and vivid fresh green, is as beautiful an addition to a dining table as a vase of flowers.

5

6

5 A central pillar partially dividing the kitchen and dining room is the perfect spot for propping up a large work of art, adding a splash of colour to the area.

6 In the stairway that runs off the kitchen, metal rails and supports have a raw, industrial feel. This is tempered, however, by a wrap of luxurious leather that's gentle on the hands. A ship's porthole makes an unusual feature.

7 These snug, round armchairs are a cosy place for an after-dinner coffee. With their front legs on castors, they're easy to move around. Their gentle contours and simple fabric covers work well in this tranquil, pared-down room.

bedrooms

Inspirational spaces for relaxation

Despite the increasingly frequent need for a bedroom to serve also as a study, exercise area or even a sitting room, its primary purpose will always be for rest and repose – a tranquil environment in which you can escape from the demands of daily life.

A soft but supportive bed, crisp cotton sheets and plenty of cosy blankets: what could be nicer when you need to relax and recharge?

When aiming to achieve a sense of calm and quiet, there may be little you can do to alter the size and basic architecture of your bedroom, but you can make the most of the available space by keeping walls and floor coverings as simple as possible, in soft, matt colours. Using natural materials is best, not just because they look and feel good, but also because some synthetic materials emit low-level toxic fumes.

Whether it's a metal frame or a straightforward wooden plinth, the bed is, of course, the focal point, and your mattress should be the best quality you can afford – firm but not too hard. In general, concentrate on comfort and convenience – a padded headboard, a spacious bedside table, lighting that can be dimmed for intimacy but is bright enough for reading by or applying make-up, full-length mirrors, a roomy dressing area and plenty of adaptable storage. Crisp, cool bedlinen, piles of soft pillows and layers of thick blankets or quilts make this room a place where you'll always feel energized and at ease.

1 In this unfussy bedroom background colours are restricted to ivory and golden browns; the striped blanket in complementary shades provides the main decorative interest. Scrubbed floorboards are an excellent choice for allergy sufferers, but if you prefer a little more comfort underfoot you could add a bedside rug. The long stool at the foot of the bed is handy for folded-back blankets or thrown-down clothes.

the irresistible luxury
of utter simplicity

A bedroom you'll want to be in even when you're not sleeping: the sophisticated palette of white, taupe and chocolate, and interesting details such as button fastenings and chunky, contrasting blanket stitch, make this room gorgeous to look at and sumptuous in feel. And it's not expensive to achieve, either – the basics are extremely simple and the only potential difficulty might be in limiting one's possessions in order to eliminate clutter and allow the subtlety of this look to really stand out.

Upholstered headboards can look old-fashioned and frumpy, but they're undeniably useful when it comes to sitting up in bed reading or watching TV. Here's a good solution: minimal padding, a clean square shape and a linen throw that coordinates with blanket and pillows. Plain white-painted walls, white bedlinen and a white lampshade to match make a subtle backdrop for the patinated oak floorboards and simple furniture.

Next to the bed the slatted table has room for everything: books, a light, clock-radio, family photo and even a terracotta pot containing a houseplant – a healthy addition to a bedroom since plants extract carbon dioxide from the air and give off oxygen, making a good night's sleep even more restorative.

1 Contrast borders, whether on pillows, cushions, curtains or valances, always look well-finished. It's also a useful way of picking up other colours or patterns in a scheme without looking overdone. Here, the choice of imitation horn buttons is a particularly chic touch.

2 A bedside table can be a simple wooden frame, as here, or a more complex piece with drawers and perhaps a cupboard. Or you could use a flat-seated chair or stool which, with the addition of a cushion, would make a useful extra seat. The ideal height for a bedside table is approximately level with the top of the mattress.

3 Placing a minimal full-length mirror on castors means it can be easily pushed out of the way when not in use.

4 A simple colour scheme shows off soft textures and quirky details such as bold blanket stitching.

a modern take on minimalism: leather, plaid and chrome

For some reason bedrooms are often considered a purely feminine preserve, and therefore decorated as such. There's no need, however, for a bedroom to be a romantic, flouncy, floral affair – a masculine edge can be just as attractive as well as offering all the necessary elements of undisturbed quiet and calm.

Leather and metal are both generally seen as having masculine characteristics; in this bedroom a chunky wardrobe handle echoes the look of a sculptural chair (by Finnish designer Alvar Aalto) positioned by the window. To further emphasize the sophisticated, masculine feel, lengths of men's suiting have been hung as dark curtains over a Venetian blind, while similar fabrics in a palette of varied greys have been made into pillows and bedlinen. A tall bedside lamp, modern and minimal in matt chrome, has all the right attributes, and no extraneous objects have been allowed to impinge on this effortlessly toned space. That's not to say the owners have no possessions: in fact, plenty of things have been hidden on shelves built into a large panel that stands at the head of the bed. Not only does it screen the wardrobe and dressing area but, with a narrow horizontal slit cut to mirror the width of the bed, it also doubles as an ingenious storage space for books, magazines and other bedside necessities.

1 The handle of this sliding wardrobe door is agreeably solid and tactile, as well as being functional and attractive.

2 (Overleaf) If you don't have fixed lamps above the bed, a hinged-arm light is a good choice as it can be adjusted when required. Whatever version you opt for, make sure you are able to switch it off without getting out of bed. It's best to have a variety of lights in a bedroom: bright lights for general illumination, dimmed ones for a more restful mood, and specific lighting for reading, dressing and personal grooming.

3 (Overleaf) Window dressings should be capable of filtering light and, when necessary, blocking it out completely. A Venetian blind, covered by a gathered length of fabric, is an ideal way of achieving a practical and unobtrusive look.

1

3

an easy calmness that combines old and new

There's a definite air of ordered indulgence about this bedroom. Its almost puritanically simple colour palette and seemingly casual combination of old and new pieces create a wonderful calmness and an atmosphere that's cosy and fresh, inspiring yet understated.

Mixing classic and contemporary furnishings frequently seems a risky prospect, but it's unavoidable if you want to incorporate gifts from family or friends or treasures that you've collected. The trick, as here, is to unify your scheme by choosing colours, textures, shapes and proportions that complement and even echo one another, and to allow the occasional quirky object to stand out and show off its own attributes. Keep walls and floors plain and reduce clutter with plenty of storage: in this room, for example, capacious custom-built cupboards eliminate mess, while their frosted-glass fronts keep the feel open and airy. The satiny metal handles catch the light, making attractive features in their own right.

1 Bedlinen made of heavy cotton and warm, thick wool is both luxurious and practical.

2 (Overleaf) Sand-coloured walls make a plain backdrop to a blue-and-white colour scheme which is at once deeply classic and bang up-to-date. In this room pieces from different periods are mixed with a confidence that ensures a look that is both individual and skilfully coherent.

2

3

3 Brushed stainless steel has a lovely finish that's good to look at and pleasant to the touch.

4 The frosted glass doors of these made-to-measure units give a mysterious hint as to their contents without looking untidy. Never underestimate the amount of storage you'll need in a bedroom; mixing open shelves with enclosed cupboards and drawers allows your favourite objects to be on show.

5 (Overleaf) Pale birch cabinets complement stripped floorboards and a sand-coloured wall. In keeping with the restricted shades used in this room, the photographs (black and white, of course) are displayed in simple frames made of matching wood.

6 (Overleaf) A floor-to-ceiling blind screens a pair of French windows. If you have a large window area to cover, a wooden Venetian blind may be more affordable than a fabric curtain, and has subtle, modern impact.

adaptable children's space for sleeping, playing and studying

A child's bedroom has different requirements from those of an adult's. As well as being a restful place to sleep, it needs to provide fun space for recreation, drawing and reading, and perhaps an ordered area for doing homework – all in safety and without overflowing into adjoining rooms in the rest of the house.

If the room is to last from nursery to teenage years, it needs to be adaptable – cuddly teddies or pink princesses will soon become outdated. Paint the walls a neutral colour and keep furniture simple: solid, sturdy timber is ideal, and if you can put anything on castors, it makes the room even more flexible. Easy-clean wood floors are a good choice, covered with a large rug for softness and to muffle noise, while plenty of storage is essential. Here, the high beds create room underneath for storage and a secret 'den'; all necessary colour is provided by the bedlinen and an exuberant display of toys and paintings.

1 Safety must be paramount in a child's room. A non-slip rug, security rails on high beds, lockable castors and furniture that can't be easily toppled over are all important features here. For extra tidiness, abandoned toys could easily be swept up into a large box or basket.

bathrooms

Practical spaces for pure indulgence

Necessary function or sensory indulgence? There are two schools of thought when it comes to bathing, with brisk efficiency at one end of the spectrum and utter hedonism at the other. But why not enjoy both possibilities? The modern bathroom can be a well-appointed and agreeable place in which to cleanse both body and mind, a room which is perfectly practical and also a haven in which to relax, reflect and refresh.

The modern bathroom combines efficiency with blissful luxury. Beautiful fittings, restful colours, a space-enhancing layout and a warm ambience will make it the most sought-after room in the house.

Get it right and your bathroom will possess a sense of nurture and well-being; get it wrong and it could be either showy and vulgar or cold and institutional. Whether it's large or small, contemporary or classic, brightly coloured or plain and simple, it's how it feels that counts, in terms of the emotions it evokes and, more literally, in textures and temperatures against bare skin.

The starting point when designing a bathroom is usually a scaled drawing to help you choose and arrange bath/shower, basin and lavatory – consulting experts at this stage would be a wise idea. They can help, too, with planning the heating, lighting and ventilation, all of which have an important bearing on the room's look as much as its functions. Fittings are available in a multitude of styles (and prices), but simplicity is often the

1 An all-white bathroom has a certain purity and a wide appeal. In this case, although fairly spartan in appearance, the room is saved from being overwhelmingly austere by the warmth of the irregularly coloured, softly worn quarry tiles on the floor. You could soften harsh white walls further by hanging thick towels over the bath rail or a bright image on the wall.

best option: bear in mind that plain, inexpensive designs can look wonderful when teamed with interesting accessories. Walls and floors need to be waterproof, storage should be well thought out and there are important safety considerations such as non-slip flooring and steamproof light fittings. That said, however, there is still endless potential, from the purity of white tiling to coarse natural matting, from the solidity of a stone basin to a sleek hi-tech tap, for creating a room that reflects a certain attitude of mind and offers an experience that is comfortable and convenient, warm and welcoming, clean and calm.

2 Gloss-painted tongue-and-groove panelling makes an attractive splashback; the roughly plastered wall above is covered in mould-resistant matt paint. Such differing textures are effective in this simple room, and the ceramic basin with chrome plumbing is unpretentious and eye-catching.

3 Vibrant cobalt-blue mosaic tiles and sunny yellow paintwork contrast with a hospital-style sink and tap and a solid timber surround. This mix shows a sense of humour and personality.

4 Limited colours in contrasting patterns give this guest cloakroom a coherent look. Its classical fittings are generously sized and comfortably solid.

5 This is a clever idea: a cherry-wood mirror frame features an integral shelf for keeping essentials close at hand and displaying shells, soaps and plants. A good mirror is essential in a bathroom (usually placed over the hand basin) and electric heating pads behind it will prevent it from steaming up.

129

plain and simple for purity of style

Waterproof, stainproof, tough and durable, ceramic tiles have always been a favourite choice for bathroom walls and floors. They're also convenient to clean, and their glazed surface reflects and increases light as well as being pleasantly smooth to the touch. These two guest bathrooms – one utterly minimal and almost ascetic, the other vibrant and characterful – demonstrate how some surprisingly different effects can be achieved by using the same basic material.

Square, white, machine-made tiles are an inexpensive bathroom standard, and make a useful, unfussy background to all sorts of decorative schemes. Because they can look bland, however, it's best to combine them with other colours, materials or shapes – tongue-and-groove, painted plaster, mosaic, mirror or glass, for example. Overleaf, a black-and-white chequerboard effect adds dramatic interest to the floor of a white-walled shower room, while the curving wall and archway create an intriguing interplay of geometric forms.

In another guest bathroom, by contrast, the vividly coloured tiles are handmade, and, as a result, slightly irregular in shape and surface. The walls have been painted tomato red, but these rather rustic features are juxtaposed with a gloriously smooth and shiny basin which, in turn, is set into a thick wooden plinth. The overall result is a pleasurable variety of textures that combines the best of modern and traditional.

1 There's a satisfying regularity to an evenly tiled bathroom, whether white or any other colour. This understated corner plays off the smooth-on-smooth combination of glass on tile against the mirror's sandblasted edge – as well as juxtaposing different geometric shapes.

1

2 When using tiles, remember that the grout between them has a huge effect on their finished appearance: it's usual to pick a similar tone that will blend in, but sometimes, as here, it's fun to use a contrasting shade to create an unusual effect.

3 This room has a cool, pristine atmosphere, but need not necessarily feel cold to the touch. Underfloor heating is both inconspicuous and luxurious, and a heated towel rail, hung with fluffy towels, is an alternative source of heat.

calm and serene: a classic look offers timeless delight

To create a warm, harmonious and luxurious bathroom, classic fittings and the mellow colours of natural materials are a simple and understated choice, with universal, timeless appeal.

The owners of this family bathroom, for example, have used polished limestone as a flooring, in a dark colour which provides an attractive base for the honey-coloured, Italian handmade tiles that envelop almost the entire room. A champagne-coloured, Edwardian basin and bath taps are practical and good-looking without being showy, the sort of thoughtful detail that makes an enormous difference to a room in which feel is as important as function. Around the basin a simple cherrywood cabinet with sandblasted glass doors conceals the plumbing as well as hiding unattractive cleaning equipment and other necessities.

Storage is often neglected in bathrooms, but it's a vital element and should never be left as an afterthought – it makes all the difference between a messy and cluttered space and a room that works well and allows you to unwind in total serenity. You'll need open shelves and enclosed cupboards, perhaps some discreet drawers or a few pretty baskets, and, of course, plenty of rails on which to pile your thickest, softest towels.

1 Traditional taps possess inherent elegance and work well in many types of bathroom. You can buy authentic reproductions or, if you prefer, original, reconditioned fittings from a reclamation yard – if you opt for the latter, however, do ensure that they are compatible with modern plumbing.

2

2 The complex workings of an Edwardian 'telephone' shower and taps make a fascinating structural study. The fitting has graceful form and attractive solidity – something to aim for even if you prefer a more modern design.

3 A clever storage solution: tiled recesses, one with mirrored doors and two more with cherrywood shelves that match the cabinet below. They take up no extra space and provide room for all sorts of bathroom accessories.

4 + **5** (Overleaf) Turn off the lights and enjoy the flickering glow of an assortment of candles and nightlights. Keep towels and other accessories plain to emphasize a tranquil atmosphere, then add some gentle background music for the ultimate in indulgent evenings.

understated effect with wood, stone and steel

1 A corner where mirror, concrete and wood converge: in this subtle scheme each material enhances the qualities of the others. Excellent workmanship is essential for such simplicity to work. The accessories, although attractive in themselves, are as understated as their surroundings.

Even the smallest accessory can have great impact in a bathroom, and choosing the right pieces gives satisfying visual unity or variety, as well as providing useful storage space. Here, the emphasis is on the tactile quality of brushed stainless steel and polished oak, from lavatory and basin to coordinating soap dish and tooth mug.

Though at first this loo may seem aggressively modern, combining it with wood and stone, their colours and grains left natural and untreated, makes for an interesting rather than industrial feel.

One wall – very practically – is fitted with edge-to-edge mirror; the other is made of polished concrete, which has a patina similar to plaster. Deep solid-oak shelves stretch from floor to ceiling, while a matching cabinet fits around the hand basin and from wall to wall. The whole ensemble looks simple, but that's the trick: this sophisticated room is effective because it's been thought through in every detail and finished to the highest possible standard.

2 Modern taps can be as elegant as their traditional counterparts – this refined pillar with its gently arched spout sits sleekly over a shiny steel bowl.

3 Bare concrete is an unusual surface for an interior wall, but has an interesting patina and is becoming increasingly fashionable. In a bathroom, however, it needs to be sealed against moisture.

4 This stainless steel lavatory is almost futuristic in design, yet it sits on classic stone flags and has a warm wood seat. In this bathroom, where there are no distracting colours, frills or fancies, the quality of the materials used becomes even more important.

4

garden rooms

Outdoor spaces for enlightened living

In an increasingly fast-paced, stressful world, it's no wonder that more and more people are taking up gardening, moving to the country or simply grabbing every possible opportunity to enjoy the delights of the great outdoors. For busy city-dwellers, bringing a little bit of nature into an

Make the next space you add to your home an outdoor retreat, where natural light, abundant greenery and the changing seasons create the decoration.

apartment is literally like a breath of fresh air – and, wherever you live, creating a whole garden room will increase not only the size of your home, but also its living potential.

It could be a patio with a fold-away awning, a tiny balcony with just enough room for a breakfast table and a couple of chairs, a ramshackle glass shed, a roof terrace, a fully fledged conservatory or even a purpose-built sauna: there are no rules as to what form an outdoor room should take. It can be as simple or sophisticated as you like. Its underlying principles are only that it is open to the elements yet also protected from them; that plants, flowers, fruit and vegetables are a prominent feature; and that its atmosphere is robust and unpretentious. Made comfortable with simple, rustic furnishings, this is a room from which to observe the changing seasons and enjoy the sounds and scents of nature; a peaceful haven in which to retreat to a less frenetic way of life.

1 At one end of this first-floor city kitchen a pair of folding doors leads onto a small but sunny balcony, where a table and bench can just be fitted. A weathered flowerpot provides a charming contrast to the smooth, golden wood of the furniture.

an inspiring approach to modern rustic

1 Natural wood looks at home inside and outside this glass and steel shelter. Its furniture is robust enough for all-year-round use, yet is not too heavy in appearance.

Despite its confidently modern appearance, the shape of this outdoor sauna is based on that of traditional models, and the light simplicity of its design means that it does not detract from the idyllic rural setting. From inside the glazed sunroom, nearby trees give the illusion of surrounding walls, while, outside, the large overhanging eaves provide welcome shade on all four sides of the structure.

The right flooring is crucial for a garden room: anything too soft and luxurious will both look and feel wrong – what's needed is something tough and hard-wearing but not too urban or industrial. Generally, stone is a good choice, as are terracotta tiles, timber decking or woven matting such as sisal or coir. The owner of this sunroom chose randomly cut stone flags which are both rustic and practical, their dark colour contrasting with the golden shade of the slatted furniture. A restricted palette – shades of charcoal and honey, no materials other than wood, stone, steel and glass, the only textiles towels and dressing gowns – maintains a pleasant purity here, a lesson in harmonizing light and dark, sun and shade, heat and cold, inside and out.

2 (Overleaf) The unusual 45-degree incline of the stone floor behind the sauna benches was inspired by Maori culture and also the Catalan architect Antonio Gaudí. The end result is simple, yet has striking visual appeal.

unpretentious dining: a little roughness around the edges

Like having a picnic, but with the added bonus of shelter from sun, wind or showers, eating in an outdoor room is always an enjoyable experience. This quirky greenhouse (though new, its tumbledown appearance is reminiscent of a setting from a fairy tale) is regularly used for long, leisurely lunches and suppers with family and friends, making a wonderful change from more conventional dining.

Sensibly, the owners haven't tried to turn this peaceful spot into an ultra-efficient, sophisticated room, but have allowed its appealingly rough and ready character to shine through. Only the necessary conveniences – a solid flagstone floor, a large wooden table, folding chairs, some eccentric lighting and plenty of shelving – have been added in order to enjoy outdoor entertainment in style. The room also has plenty of storage space for bottled preserves, plants and fruit and veg from the garden, all of which provide an attractive backdrop that's far nicer than any carefully planned furnishings. Jumbled with baskets, breadboards, mismatching china, a plethora of candles and the occasional blanket for chilly nights, this is an artless, unpretentious look that's at once wholesome and irresistibly pretty.

1 Despite its highly individual setting, this outdoor look could, in fact, be easily emulated indoors, using simple furnishings and a background of plants, flowers, fruit and vegetables, displayed in assorted containers. The curled brass candelabra adds an unexpected touch of glamour and intimacy, particularly in an outdoor setting.

2 Plain china, bone-handled cutlery and a checked napkin have timeless appeal. The glass tumbler is more contemporary, but the whole setting is understated enough to work in town or country, indoors or out.

3 Made of unpainted reclaimed wood and glass, this greenhouse doubles as a dining room, but its function as storeroom and plant propagator is undisguised.

4 A chic blue and white ceramic vase is played down by adding a country-style arrangement of white blooms. The assortment of different elements in the room is what makes it so attractive – trying to match everything would take away some of its magic.

5 Enjoying long, leisurely mealtimes in the company of good friends becomes even more memorable in a simple outdoor setting such as this.

6

6 The rewards of gardening are not just in tending plants and watching them grow but in picking, cooking and eating the results of your labours. The produce of this large, well-cared-for garden makes a mouth-watering display; its rich colours and fascinating textures are as radiant as any work of art.

7 On a floor of softly worn flagstones, a fold-away chair invites an occupant. In the background, glass jars of preserved fruit glow like jewels in the sunshine. A similar effect could be achieved by running a plain wooden shelf across a kitchen window.

GENERAL/DEPARTMENT STORES

Andrew Martin 200 Walton St, London
SW3 2JL tel: (020) 7225 5100
The Conran Shop 81 Fulham Rd, London
  SW3 6RD tel: (020) 7589 7401 * ✓
Designers Guild 267–277 Kings Rd,
  London SW3 5EN tel: (020) 7351 5775
The General Trading Company
  144 Sloane St, London SW1X 9BL
  tel: (020) 7730 0411
Geoffrey Drayton 85 Hampstead Rd,
  London NW1 2PL tel: (020) 7387 5840
Heal's 196 Tottenham Court Rd, London
W1P 9LD tel: (020) 7636 1666 *
Ikea (020) 8208 5600 *
InHouse 28 Howe St, Edinburgh
  EH3 6TG tel: (0131) 225 2888 *
Jerry's Home Store 163 Fulham Rd,
  London SW3 6SN tel: (020) 7581 0909 * ✓
Muji 187 Oxford St, London W1R 1AJ
  tel: (020) 7437 7503 *
Nicole Farhi Home 17 Clifford St, London
W1X 1RG tel: (020) 7494 9051

resources

R.O.O.M shops and
other outlets from
which to source the
Modern Comfort look

FURNITURE

Castle Gibson (reconditioned office
  furniture) 106a Upper St, London N1 12N
  tel: (020) 7704 0927
Highly Sprung 310 Battersea Park Rd,
  London SW11 3BU tel: (020) 7924 1124 *
Hitch Mylius tel: (020) 8443 2616 *
The Holding Company 245 Kings Rd,
  London SW3 5EL tel: (020) 7352 1600 ✓
Lloyd Davies 14 John Dalton St,
  Manchester M2 6JR tel: (0161) 832 3700
Purves & Purves 83 Tottenham Court Rd,
  London W1P 9HD tel: (020) 7580 8223 ✓
SCP 135 Curtain Rd, London EC2A 3BX
  tel: (020) 7739 1869
Viaduct 1 Summer's St, London EC1R 5BD
  tel: (020) 7278 8456

BATHROOMS

Alternative Plans 9 Hester Rd, London
SW11 4AN tel: (020) 7228 6460
Aston Matthews 141 Essex Rd,
  London N1 2FN tel: (020) 7226 7220
CP Hart 103 Regents Park Rd,
  London NW1 8UR tel: (020) 7586 9856 *
Original Bathrooms 143–145 Kew Rd,
Richmond, Surrey, TW9 2PN
  tel: (020) 8940 7554

BEDLINEN/FABRIC/WINDOW
TREATMENTS

Bruno Triplet tel: (020) 7795 0395 *
Catherine Memmi at Harvey Nichols
109 Knightsbridge, London SW1X 7RJ,
  tel: (020) 7235 5000
De Le Cuona tel: (01753) 830301 *
Eclectics Blinds tel: (01843) 852888 *
  tel: (0870) 0102211 ✓
Ian Mankin 109 Regents Park Rd, London
  NW1 8UR tel: (020) 7722 0997 * ✓
MacCulloch & Wallis 25 Dering St,
  London W1R 0BH tel: (020) 7629 0311
Manuel Canovas (Colefax & Fowler)
tel: (020) 8877 6400 *
Melin Tregwynt tel: (01348) 891225 *
The White Company tel: (020) 7385 7988 ✓

KITCHENS

Bosch tel: (020) 7253 7988 *
Bulthaup 37 Wigmore St, London
  W1H 9LD tel: (020) 7495 3663 *
Camargue tel: (01582) 699122 *
Fulham Kitchens tel: (020) 7736 6458 *
The Kitchen Design Co., 21 St Alban's
Place, London N1 0NX tel: (020) 7359 0224
Leicht Furniture tel: (01689) 836413 *
Miele Co., tel: (01235) 554455 *
Newcastle Furniture Co. (bespoke
  furniture) tel: (0191) 438 1342 *
Poggenpohl tel: (0800) 243781 *
SieMatic tel: (01438) 369251 *

LIGHTING

Aktiva 10b Spring Place, London NW5 3BH
  tel: (020) 7428 9325
Anglepoise tel: (01527) 63771 *
Babylon Design 301 Fulham Rd, London
  SW10 9QH tel: (020) 7376 7255
Best & Lloyd tel: (0121) 558 1191 *
Chelsea Lighting Design
  tel: (020) 7824 8144 *
CTO tel: (020) 8340 4593 *
John Cullen Lighting 585 Kings Rd,
  London SW6 2EH tel: (020) 7371 5400
The London Lighting Company
  135 Fulham Rd, London SW3 6RT
  tel: (020) 7589 3612

FLOORING

Amtico tel: (0800) 667766 *
Crucial Trading tel: (01562) 825200 *
Fired Earth tel (01295) 812088 *✓
First Floor 174 Wandsworth Bridge Rd,
  London SW6 2UQ tel: (020) 7736 1123
Forbo-Nairn tel: (01592) 643777 *
The Hardwood Flooring Company,
  146-152 West End Lane, London NW6 1SD
  tel: (020) 7328 8481
Junckers tel: (01376) 517512 *
Kährs tel: (01243) 778747
Roger Oates Design tel: (01531) 631611 *✓
Sinclair Till tel: (020) 7720 0031 ✓
Solid Floor Ltd. tel: (020) 7221 9166 *
Stonell tel: (01892) 833500 *
Wicanders tel: (01403) 710002 *

FINISHING TOUCHES

Allgood (door furniture) tel: (0990) 143158 *
Bisque Radiators tel: (01225) 469244 *
David Mellor Cookshop 4 Sloane Square
  London SW1W 8EE
  tel: (020) 7730 4259 * ✓
Divertimenti (kitchenware) 139 Fulham Rd,
  London SW3 6SD tel: (020) 7935 0689 *✓
Egg (contemporary craft) 36 Kinnerton St,
London SW1X 8ES tel: (020) 7235 9315
Forbes & Lomax Ltd (light switches)
  205a St John's Hill, London SW11 1TH
  tel: (020) 7738 0202 ✓

R.O.O.M SHOPS

R.O.O.M. Stockholm
Alströmergatan 20
(Box 49024)
100 28 Stockholm
tel: +46-8-692 50 00
R.O.O.M. Oslo
Ris Skolvej 1 (Vinderen)
(Postboks 87)
0319 Oslo
tel:+47-22 13 64 00

* Call for stockists/branches
✓ Mail order available